The "True Man's" Memory Book

As told to: Dawn Densmore-Parent

Dedication

"To my Family!"

Many Thanks!

Trueman

Cover Design by: Tamara Smith, UVM Print and Mail, VT

ISBN: 978-1-7342353-4-0

INTRODUCTION

This book is the result of a request from Pamela Cross that I write down my conversations with her father, Trueman Bryer (after Terry Bryer, her mother had passed) during time spent together with him from 2017 to 2021.

This book contains moments that he shared with me that he wanted to record for his posterity. This is what he told me. I have presented his memories in the order of his life, with some of his miscellaneous memories at the end.

Cry and laugh, as you enjoy reading about the events experienced by this remarkable man, Trueman Bryer!

Dawn Densmore-Parent

Contents

Chapter 1 - The BRYER Memorial

This book contains the memories of many things that occurred throughout my life. To get to the 'beginning' most often we must start at the 'end' – because the 'end' is directly connected to the 'beginning'. It is truly when I 'look back' upon the events of my life, that I can clearly see the hand of the Lord moving to enable us to experience so many remarkable events. Each of my life's adventures began with a 'vision'. Each required action on my part, and each was followed by a: 'Then" result. One of the last things Terry and I did, was to decide that we wanted to have a memorial stone.

The Stone Polisher

Terry's father had been a stone polisher. He polished not the entire stone, but the ridges of the stone. The ridges are the most difficult 'part" of the stone to work with. But he was an expert in his craft and because of this, Terry was drawn to carved stones. She had watched him and seen him turn a stone that looked like 'nothing' into something 'magical' and 'amazing'! I used to joke with her, "Terry takes nothing for granite!"

Our Design

When we talked about having our own memorial stone, we knew immediately what we wanted on it. We both loved the lake and so we wanted to have the lake on our stone. So, I sat down at our table and created a drawing that included mountains, the sun setting on the water and the Lake, and then put our name "Bryer" right in the middle of the lake.

My Simple Drawing

We took my simple drawing to a dealer and placed it on the table and waited for their reaction. We were told they could create the image of my drawing on a stone, and they would work to make a print image for our approval. We left, and then waited with excitement for their proof print. Finally, they called. They had an image for our approval, and we went with excitement to go see it. But what was 'seen' was NOT even close to what I had given them.

Their Objections

First, they did not want to put the name 'BRYER" in the middle of the water, and they had changed everything within my drawing. I insisted "BRYER" be placed within the 'water' on the stone. They had also added the 'moon' and removed the light of the sun setting in the water. We were told the 'moon' should be in the picture. We did not agree! We wanted it to be the 'sun setting' with its reflection on the water! The 'sun setting on the water' represented the 'end' of our lives on this earth, not the 'moon'! I immediately made another 'sketch' with all the modifications that we wanted.

Our Success

Finally, their second drawing was done. That drawing returned with what is currently on the stone! We both were very pleased with the results.

The Stone

Next was the stone itself. Terry and I wanted a 'dark' colored stone rather than a 'grey' stone. When we told the dealer, we wanted a dark stone, he told us there was a dark stone on a 'boat' headed our way from Italy. It had been ordered, but the person who ordered it, no longer wanted it! And the next was the best: "If we were interested, he could give us 'that stone' at a substantially reduced rate."

The Size

When he told us the amount, we agreed we would purchase it – sight unseen! We were totally surprised by the 'size' of the stone when it arrived. We would never have purchased a stone that was this large; however, the size of the stone turned out to be the 'perfect size' for the image we desired with the engraving of the sun, mountains, water, and reflection of the sun in the water! And yes, the name 'BRYER' is placed firmly within the center of the water, as we requested.

Faith

We lived our life doing the best we could with what we had, no matter our circumstance. Truly we trusted in God for everything.

A Heavenly Home

Terry's passing was not 'unexpected'. We knew she was struggling with health issues. But her passing was much sooner than any of us anticipated. Adjusting to her physical absence has been challenging for everyone.

Our grave site contains her 'body' – but it is faith in Jesus Christ that assures me that Terry is in heaven with the Lord where 'death' no longer 'rules', because Jesus is alive forever up there!

The Greeting

As I arrived at the grave site, I threw Terry a kiss and said, "Hi Terry, I miss you and love you, tons!"

The Flowers

The flowers my daughter Pam planted were shaded by the stone from the hot sun and doing wonderfully in that location, banked by gladiolas on either side. I exclaimed, "Pam did a great job with the flowers!"

As we sat, we talked about 'Terry' and the fact that she is with the Lord in heaven. The gravesite is where her body now 'rests' but I will see her again.

The Surprise

The visit to see the flowers around the gravestone produced a BIG surprise. As we got ready to leave, Dawn snapped a picture of the stone with the flowers and turned to show me that picture. What a 'surprise' we saw! The camera had caught our reflection! Dawn said, "Trueman, this image is showing us that we are 'truly' with her 'even now' – right now! We appear to be 'with her' within the stone – as though we are in that 'next dimension' with her at this very moment." I smiled. As I walked away, I turned and waved and said, "Goodbye for now!"

Reflection

Our current beautiful world is not predictable in any way. Faith requires us to live one day at a time.

Footnote: Terry's Parents are buried in Montpelier, VT - Trueman's parents are buried in Northfield Falls, VT

Chapter 2 - Terry

Terry's parents lived in Berlin, about 6 or 7 miles from my parents' home in Northfield. When we visited with the kids, we would go to visit both places to see them.

How Terry and I Met

I met Terry when I was in the Navy. I had been invited to go to a dance at "Wayside" located in the Montpelier- Barre area. They held dances there at that time and one of my friends had asked me to go with him. He knew Terry's older sister. And Terry was there at that dance with her older sister. Terry and I hit it off right away, but it was difficult for me to see her because of my Navy position.

The Letters

We both would write letters when I was on a ship out of Norfolk, Virginia. Then I got stationed out of Boston, Massachusetts, and I was assigned to the Fargo Building in South Boston, a major Navy Relay Station.

The Art of Hitch-Hike

At that time, you could 'hitch-hike'. I would walk to Cambridge, MA to find Route 4 and then I could hitch a ride to White River Junction, VT. Then I would hitch a ride from White River Junction to Montpelier, VT.

One night, I had a hard time getting a ride, and a truck took me to St. Johnsbury, VT and then I still had 80 miles to hitch into Montpelier, VT. It was a long, long night, but I got there in the morning!

Church

Once I arrived, I started to walk down the street. Low and behold, Terry and her family came walking along that very street right towards me! They were going to church! So, I just joined them and walked to church with them.

The Return Home

After my visit, one of the boys would take me home so I could visit with my folks. Then, I would arrange to go back and meet Terry later in the day.

Wearing My Uniform

My dad would give me $5 to take the bus, for me to get back to Massachusetts. I wore my blue uniform and my white hat. Cars would go screeching past and then stop and back up to pick me up. I was told many times, had it not been for that 'white hat' they would have never stopped.

The Ring

It wasn't long before I mentioned marriage to Terry, and I worked to save money so I could buy her an engagement ring. We ate all our meals at her parents' home. We did not eat at restaurants but worked to save and to be as economical as possible. Each weekend it was the same. I tried to come home every weekend that I didn't have a work assignment.

Chapter 3 – Trueman -Growing Up

Swimming as a Kid

When I was growing up, we would swim in the Dog River in Northfield. The swimming hole was about a mile away and we would go with our bikes to get there. Typically, there would be 25-30 kids swimming there. It had a gravel bed, but it was deep enough to swim in. I would go with my brother. That is where I taught myself how to swim. I never saw the ocean until I went into the Navy.

The Boy Scouts and my Paper Route

My life was busy for sure. I enjoyed the Boy Scouts. I became an Eagle Scout. And when I was not participating in the Boy Scouts, I was busy with other things. When I was older, I continued to be involved in the Boy Scouts as an active Leader of different teams for many years.

The Paper Route

I had an early morning paper route in Northfield once a week.

The Contest

The Drug Store put on a contest and put up two prizes: 1 bicycle for a girl and 1 bicycle for a boy. The ones who won the contest were the ones that got the most points. We had to really work hard for it, and I wanted that bike! I did win the bike, and it was the only bike I ever had as a kid, but had I been paid 10 cents an hour for the hours I worked for that bike, I could have purchased six of them!

First Grade

My First-grade school class was in Randolph and my teacher was Miss Rice – she was young and pretty – and I was in love with her!

Second Grade

Second grade was also in Randolph.

Third Grade

After Second grade, then my family moved to Northfield, so my 3rd grade class was with Misty Divine. She was husky and what was then called 'an old maid' because she never married. Back then you had to be 'unmarried' to be able to teach.

Fourth Grade

I do not seem to recall my Fourth-grade teacher!

Fifth Grade

My Fifth-grade teacher was Miss McNama.

Sixth Grade

My Sixth-grade class had a widow who had been married, but when her husband died, she became a teacher.

My School Friend

My Sixth-grade teacher had a son named Donald, and we were friends. He went into the Army and was in action during WWII. He and I fooled around a lot on bicycles. He was a real 'dare devil' and could do amazing things with his bike, that I wouldn't even try to do.

Donald

Donald was quite a bit older than me. One day the school had a visit from a Telegraph Officer. Back then, a man was available on call and when a Telegram came, he would be called to go and deliver it.

Delivery of News

There was a knock on the school door, and that Telegraph Officer handed a Telegraph message to my teacher. That telegraph message gave news that Donald had died. Once he had handed her the message, he just left.

It was a horrible thing to happen, but the way they notified my teacher was even more horrible. The way it was done was very insensitive for she was a widow with an only son. The Telegraph Office should have notified a minister to go and to speak to her.

How I Got Zapped

When I was about 10 years old or less, I had a friend who had a telegraph set with a battery in it that would make it 'beep' back and forth. We were playing together with that set, and as I held one wire in my mouth, I plugged the other wire in – and BANG! I got hit bad and that ended the fun that day for sure!

Golf

I never liked golf. My work buddies loved golf! But I just never got 'into' it! But one time when I went on a trip, I played. I would play when I went on trips. That one time I won the pot of $200-300. I actually 'played better' when I didn't play much, than my buddies who were playing all the time.

Was I Not Counting. .?

I was in the Navy 3 years, 3 months, and 19 days. I was listed as being for 'minority' and as 'minority' they had to discharge me before I turned 21. That had to be done on Nov. 21, 1948.

Our Marriage

I was discharged on September 19, 1948. Terry and I were married on October 9,1948. Terry's birthday was October 8th.

The Honeymoon Car

I purchased a 1934 Ford convertible coupe for $50 from my brother-in-law and we went to Boston and Rhode Island for our honeymoon. We stayed with relatives, as hotels were too expensive. The car had a rumble seat that opened for seating two people. My brother-in-law had purchased it for $50 and he sold it to me for the same amount!

TRAINS

I never rode a train until I enlisted in the Navy. My first train ride was to Springfield, Massachusetts.

Our First Home!

Our first home was an apartment we rented in Berlin, VT.

. MEMORIES OF PIVOTALBE MOMENTS

President John F. Kennedy

When President John F. Kennedy was shot, we lived in St. Albans. I had been working nights and woke up to find that out!

The news at the time reported that he was alive and in the hospital. But President Kennedy was likely dead at the time the news was broadcast.

Vice President L.B. Johnson was flown around the country, and finally there was the announcement that John F. Kennedy was dead.

L.B Johnson was sworn into office as the country mourned the loss.

New York City Twin Towers

In 2001, I was sitting in my chair at camp watching the news when the first plane hit the tower, and I didn't think much about it when it happened. It made me remember a time during WWII when I was visiting my sister who was in the WAVES in New York at Hunter College. I had travelled down with a friend to visit her and when we were there, as we were standing in front of the station, there were 3 bomber planes that were in the fog, and they hit buildings.

So, planes flying through bad weather had hit buildings in NY before, and I thought this was what had happened again – a plane had gotten blinded and hit the tower.

In 2001, when the 2nd plane hit the 2nd tower, I knew this was **NOT** the same thing. The real men on the fourth plane were the heroes of the day, when they knew what was happening and determined to make sure their plane did not hit the White House. Those men on the plane knew they were as good as 'dead'. They knew they were going to die. The lead person called his wife and then a group on the plane took over the plane and found a vacant lot to put the plane down. They were heroes for sure!

The Palmer Farm -Route 7 Georgia Vermont

I remember being on the Gardner Palmer farm in Georgia, Vermont because I sold insurance to Theresa Palmer. (The farm is still insured with State Farm.) I remember Dayle, and the other Palmer girls.

The Georgia Shore Road is not the same at all. My insurance sales caused me to travel the roads all over, but things have changed a lot since those days. Lots of new houses have been built along the roads that were never there before.

What has been done to the Palmer farm is truly amazing. So many flower gardens and so well kept. Hard to believe how beautiful everything is on the farm now. When I was there before, it was a working farm! Now, the farm looks more like a resort! There are so many gardens!

Chapter 4 - My Grand Parents & Aunt

Trueman Genealogy

My mother's full name was "Ethel Goodwin Bryer" and she was born in New Hampshire.

My Dad's name was "Charles Truman Bryer".

My sister was Mildred, known as 'Millie" - She was born in Maine.

My brother was Adelfred, we called him "Del."

I was 4 years older than Del and four years younger than Millie.

I was born in Woodsville, New Hampshire on November 15, 1928.

My Mom had a sister named Silvia, known to me as Aunt Silvia.

My favorite uncle was Uncle Raymond.

I had a cousin Normand was 6'3" and 200+ lbs., -he was twice my age.

Visits

I went to visit my mother's folks with my Mom and Dad who lived in Freemont, New Hampshire. We had an old car, and it was at least a half day ride to get there. They lived in Dover Foxcroft, NH. Dad's folks lived up in Maine and we went there only once or twice. Trips were done every 7-8 years so they could 'catch up' on what was going on.

Children – Then . . .

Children, then, were not to be 'seen' or 'heard' on those visits. It was time for the adults to 'talk'. I liked my mother's parents very much!

The Game

I liked to go and visit my Mom's parents. They would do 'jack knife' swapping. Each would put a 'jack knife in their hand so that you could only see the ends of the knives. Then you both would hold out an empty hand and each would 'drop' their knife at the same time into the other person's empty hand. The goal was to give your 'worst' knife to someone and to get a better knife from them! It was a 'blind' swap and you got to keep the knife that you got!

The Knife

When my grandfather was getting old, he decided to give two knives away, one to me and one to my brother.

We got to pick the knife we would get. He allowed me to pick first because I was older. I will never forget this or his mustache. He had an extraordinary jack knife which was a large size, close to 6" long when it was folded up and closed. I still have it today and I used it on several deer. I was probably 14-15 years old at the time, and it was an expensive knife. I have looked it up on the internet since that become available and was able to find one just like it. This one has a black wooden handle. The knife came from my mother's father. The year of manufacture was 1894. You could sharpen it and it would peel off the hair on your arm, it is very sharp! I think if my grandfather knew 'now' the care I took of it, he would be pleased! He got that knife in a 'knife swap.'

I have some other special knives, one for Andy and a second knife for Patrick as well.

Millie

My sister Millie went into the military and served as a Flight Aviation Instructor. She taught pilots how to fly using instruments only. They used a flight simulator, and when pilots opened the door, some fell onto the floor, because the simulator plane was 'upside down'. Then, they knew they had failed the flight test. I considered her to be 'eccentric' because of her exciting life with teaching aviation flight.

Perk

One of the benefits of her position was being able to catch a 'lift' with 2-3 other pilots who were taking a plane on some jump location. She would board to tag along. Once the pilots knew that she was a 'flight instructor', they would invite her into the cockpit to 'fly' the plane for them. She loved doing this and did it often. She flew to many different locations and always had exciting stories to tell about her adventures.

Chapter 5 - Polly the Parrot and Cocoa

Polly the Parrot

My Mother's brother, my Uncle Perley (Goodwin) bought a parrot for his mother and father who were my grandmother and grandfather. The parrot was green and yellow and orange and had other colors mixed in, it was a very colorful bird! He brought the bird, the cage and everything needed to care for the parrot. The parrot was just 1 year old when she was given to my family. I was not a baby, but I was just a child – a very young child. They named the parrot "Polly", but we were unsure if it was a male or a female. My mother Ethel took care of Polly, but we all pitched in to feed her. She had to change the papers in the bottom of the cage 2 times a day. We were warned not to stick our fingers into the cage. If the parrot bit you, it could break a finger! The parrot did break a pencil with its beak. When we were eating, Polly would take her foot and grab a 'foot' full of seed from her food bin and toss the seeds onto the floor. She knew just how to tell us she was not happy with us eating food and not giving any of our food to her! She wanted people food!

The Switchboard.

My grandparents had a contract to run the telephone switchboard in Franconia, New Hampshire. In those days, the telephone was a switchboard that was in my grandparent's house. The parrot was given 'free range' around the room where she was placed. Polly learned quickly that she could fly over and lift the lever called a 'drop' on that switchboard! Polly would land on the top of that switchboard and reach down and 'flip a switch', then quickly fly away. The Switchboard phone would then begin to buzz. Polly loved it when no one answered because then the phone would then continue to buzz. Polly would laugh 'ha ha ha'. Then, someone had to go and plug that 'drop' cord back in. But, by now, Polly had travelled way across the room. It took a long time for my grandparents to make the connection between 'how' the switch got pulled out!

Home Life

When my grandparents got too old to operate the switchboard, they moved to an open section of the duplex.

My grandparents were also getting too old to care for the parrot. My grandfather had a stick of wood that he would use to get Polly up out of the bottom of the cage to get her to go up to the swing. But Polly wanted to PLAY! When they couldn't give Polly the level of attention that she needed, it was then that my parents took Polly.

Florida Trip

My parents would take Polly in her cage in their car for their trip to Florida. Polly just loved to ride in the car. She would sit up on the dashboard and look out the front window. Once we arrived, when we went to the beach, they would take the cage with Polly and place the cage on the sand. Polly loved to kick the sand around with her feet from inside the cage. She would chatter with all the people that passed by at the beach. Polly talked and entertained everyone. People would stop to talk as they passed by, as they were very excited to encounter a parrot at the beach!

Polly Talks to the Kids

Our home in Northfield had a big room with a lot of space. We set the cage on the table next to the window. Polly loved the window because she could see outside. We would open the cage door to let Polly out, and she would jump down to the floor and then walk through the house. She would go from one room to another looking for people. Polly wanted to know what was going on. Once she found us, she would shout, "Ha ha ha'. She was 'smart' to figure out and know where to find us. Polly liked being with people and she couldn't wait to see people walking down the sidewalk in front of our home. Polly would sing and holler to anyone who went by. She amazed everybody! Everybody loved that bird!

Each Saturday afternoon in the summer the window would be open. When kids walked past, as they travelled to go to the movies, Polly would talk to them. Soon the kids were arriving a half hour early so they could see Polly. Then the kids started to talk back to Polly, and Polly talked back to them! Polly loved the kids. She would sit and listen for the kids. As soon as she heard them coming, she would call out "Pretty Polly" and then hang herself upside down in her cage with one claw on the cage wire. Then she would just swing back and forth from that one claw!

The Egg

When Polly was between 70 to 80 years old, she laid an egg, very late in life. That was when we 'knew' the parrot was female and not male. The egg had no yoke in it, just a spot on the middle, and it broke. Up until then we were just not sure!

Polly's Resting Place

When my father knew Polly was not doing well, she was put in the car for a trip to St. Albans, but Polly did not make it to St. Albans. Polly died in the cage along the way. My father didn't want to bury Polly along the road. Polly had been a part of our family far too long, so he continued travelling and brought Polly to our home in St. Albans. There, we made a quality wooden box and placed her in that box. We gathered around our garden and placed her box into a special spot under a lilac bush. Then we had a little funeral service; and that is where Polly rests, under that lilac tree that blossoms every Spring!

The Cats

Cocoa was just a kitten when we got her. My brother, Del, gave our family this beautiful Himalayan/Siamese kitten. The fur was soft and luxurious and longer than a Siamese. It looked like a Siamese face but cuter. On the way home from New York, he tried to tell us he needed to go out and pee, but we didn't listen as he did pee in the car.

Cocoa was old, about 25 years, when I called the vet. The vet could not find the records. He had thrown out the cat's records because the cat was so old, he was sure Cocoa had passed. The veterinarian, Dr. Larrow, kept records for only 25 years.

Chapter 6 – My Growing Up Years

My brother and sister

I don't have very many memories of my brother, Del, who was 4 years younger. My sister, Millie, was 4 years older. Early on in my life, in my way of thinking, she was just a girl! I would find out that there is no such thing as 'just a girl'. I now say, "You do pretty good for a girl!"!

The Laundromat

My Mom and Dad lived in Northfield and managed a drycleaner business together. During the war there were rations on gas for vehicles. They had different codes: B, C, D to allow you to obtain coupons for gas. Cars were considered a luxury, so you could only get enough gas to take you to the edge of town and back; that was about it!

The Northfield Stairs!

We lived in a building that is still there in Northfield. We lived on the 2nd floor and that took 21 steps to get to the top. I made it my habit to take about 4 steps to get up and about 3 steps to go down. I would take several steps to get up and less to go down as I hung onto the rail. My Mom frowned greatly upon me doing that, but I was very agile and balanced and could do a lot of things.

The House that was a hospital (in Northfield)

Dr. Mayo owned the building. He was working on obtaining a space to set up and run a hospital in town. A woman got 'wind' of that and applied for money and found a house that could be used as a hospital which had been a single-family residence. Two of my children were born in that 'house' that had been made into a hospital. Cathy and Pam were born there. I was notified at work when each of them arrived.

Trips to Maine

The trips we made to Maine were 'all day' drives in my Dad's two-door Chevrolet sedan. It had a seat that folded up to get out. That seat was used by the milkman to put crates of milk in the car. The car was not a distance car. The springs were not quiet. We used to count cars and plates that were 'out-of-state' or 'in-state' on our trips.

Playing Cards

I do remember adults playing cards when I was growing up, but I don't remember playing cards as a boy.

My Mom's Father's Death

When my mother's father died there was a 30" snowfall. That made travelling very challenging. My Mom took a taxi to get to the train. The equipment, back then, had difficulty removing a lot of snow. The train crew knew she was coming and held off leaving until she arrived.

My Early Christmases

Most of the time I got mittens for Christmas. We got clothes when I was young, not toys. One year, my father made an overcoat for me. I would have preferred a 'store bought' coat. but I realize how much work it was for my Dad to make that coat. It was made from an Army Soldier's coat that was taken apart and downsized and put back together for me.

Bed Sheets

When I was growing up there were just two kinds of bed sheets you could buy for a bed: Bleached or 'unbleached'. The unbleached sheets were rough but inexpensive! The bleached sheets were smooth but cost more.

Skiing

I did ski at Norwich University because they had a ski tow rope, and they would let the kids in town use it. . I did odd jobs to get a good quality set of skis.

My Dad was like a beachball with arms and legs and did not ski. However late in his life he was hired to run a team of horses through the woods for logging!

Skating

We did some skating when I was a kid, so that we could 'say' that we did it, but our feet got cold, and we didn't have the best of equipment. We had a public skating rink and not many kids knew how to skate, so they would just scoot along one foot by one foot moving slowly forward

Cars

I owned a 1953 four-door Kaiser, a Studebaker Champion Sedan, a Mercury Station Wagon, a blue Volkswagen Karmann-Ghia, a Cadillac, and a Lincoln Town car.

I got the 'Ghia' from a bad driver who had to have collision insurance and couldn't afford it, so he sold the car to me. Terry and I took it to Portland, Maine, and then on the Ferry to visit Nova Scotia. It was a fun car to drive. We fueled it up in St. Albans before the trip. It could get about 40 miles per gallon.

The 'Cadillac' came from Florida. One car dealership in St. Albans had one, but they didn't want to give me a price. That made me go to another Dealership on Lake Street and he got me a Cadillac that he had driven up to St. Albans from Florida. It was new and had about 6,000 miles from its drive North. I bought it and paid for it.

The Waterbury Camp

Terry's Brother Roger married Bev McGibny, and they had a camp in Woodbury, VT, and we went and visited them at the camp several times. I used to swim out with Bev together just to get Roger going. The camp is still in Bev's family, and they recently had a 100th year anniversary to celebrate that this camp is still owned by their family.

Church

My own Dad was not a church goer. When I was growing up, I went to the Methodist Sunday School every Sunday.

I liked Rev. Arthur W. Hewett. He was a Methodist minister and a very 'unbeautiful' man, but he was a terrifically beautiful person. He gave the messages at church and others taught the Sunday School classes.

When I met Terry, her family went to a Catholic church every Sunday. So, for me to marry Terry, I became a Catholic and then took our children to Catholic church on Sundays.

Logging with My Dad

I can remember my Dad hitching up horses to take them into the woods to go logging. He would use the horses to drag the logs down to where they would be sawed, and then he would go back and get more! I was about 9 or 10 at the time, and we lived in Maine then.

My Dad's Camera

My Dad had a small camera when I was growing up. It was new technology then. It was a box camera about 4-5" wide and you had a roll of film that you would crank around into the box and then you could take a picture with it. So, there are some pictures of me when I was young.

Our First Crank Telephone

We did have a crank up telephone that my Dad had installed in his dry-cleaning shop that was a party line. When we wanted to use it, we had to go down the stairs from our 2nd story apartment. When I wanted to make a call, I had to stand on a chair to reach it.

Eavesdropping

One time when I was at a friends' house, I wanted to call and tell my Mom I would eat dinner with my friends. So, I picked up the receiver of their black and white phone and told the operator, "I want to talk to my Mom!" She asked, "Well what's your Mom's name?" There was no privacy then. Everyone knew everyone back then. When the call was connected, and you heard the phone start to ring, you could also hear about 10 people 'click, click, click,' picking up their phones to listen! You could really get them talking when you would talk on the phone about your neighbors!

The Fair

My Dad used to like to go to the Fair. He liked seeing the horse sulky racing. There was a lot required to have success with that kind of racing. The horses had to be trained <u>not</u> to gallop. The horses had to learn to 'trot' and pull the cart and driver. My Dad loved to see that. He was not into saddle racing but preferred the sulky racing track. That would bring back memories for him of his horses in the back woods of Maine.

Hunting

When I was young, one of my joys was deer hunting. We lived in Northfield, and I hunted with my Dad, and sometimes with my brother. When my brother came with us, we had to hunt near home, because he always was ready to go home soon after we began the hunt, and we wanted to be in a place where he could go home on his own, and we could continue the hunt!

Driver's License Hunting!

One year the Army Reserve had a program where they loaned Army rifles out in Vermont in different areas. You had to have a Driver's License to get a rifle, so they could track the 'loaned rifle', but anyone could obtain a rifle and go into the woods to hunt. That year, my Dad was concerned about all of the inexperienced hunters with high powered rifles in the woods. Because of these novices and the danger posed by them, my Dad told me he knew of a place that we could go. His friend told him that we could hunt at his brother's farm any time, so we headed to that farm.

The Farm

When we arrived, the farm had a woods road and we set off down that road. We got down the road and sat down to have lunch in the woods. While we ate and were sitting, we heard a strange noise. I could hear something in front of us that was bigger than a squirrel – **crunch, crunch, crunch**. We finished lunch and Dad said, "I'm going to go up the woods road to where the road splits and find a place to sit." I said, "I'm going to stay right here, as this is as good a place as any other place!"

My First Deer

My Dad set off and went and sat down about 100 yards from where I was located.

As I sat, I listened! I could hear another sound. Down over the knoll there was a swampy area, and I could hear the pulling up of feet out of the mud - a sucking sound like when you walk through mud. It was a deer that was walking below us through muddy water. Being young, I stood up to see what it was. I took two to three steps, when suddenly, the rack of a big Buck was coming up right in front of me! The deer was picking up its head, and its horns were coming towards me out of the bushes just 50 yards from me.

Quick Action

I quickly pulled my rifle up and shot him right under the neck in his 'white' spot. The bullet broke the deer's neck, but his feet were kicking and scratching the ground as he tried to get up. I ran to the deer and shot him again in the head.

My Dad heard the first shot and the second, but he didn't understand the second shot. My Dad shouted, "What's going on?" I shouted back, 'Dad! I got a buck!" The deer weighed in at 237 pounds. My Dad and I struggled that day as we pulled that deer out of the woods. The deer rack had 11 points. We had the rack mounted.

At Sixteen

I had my first deer at 16 years old! There was a shortage of meat that was available then, so that deer really helped our family through that winter season.

The Deer Rack Rating

Much later, I had a call from someone with the 'Boone and Crocket Club' who came to the house to look at the rack. He told me he had the 'day off' and wanted to see if he could give it a rating. He brought all kinds of tools to measure with and he measured the length of the Boone, and each side, as well as the thickness of the horns. He came up with a calculation of 147 on the Boone and Crocket Club Mount.

Deer Season

I continued to hunt each year, but my first deer is my most memorable experience, because I was hunting with my Dad!

Terry would say, "He plans his vacation every year during hunting season, and then he goes hunting and gets a deer the first or second day!"

I continued to hunt in those Northfield mountains because of my familiarity with the terrain and the deer trails located there. And I did not always, as she implied, get a deer every year when I hunted, but I always enjoyed the hunt!

Chapter 7 – The Navy

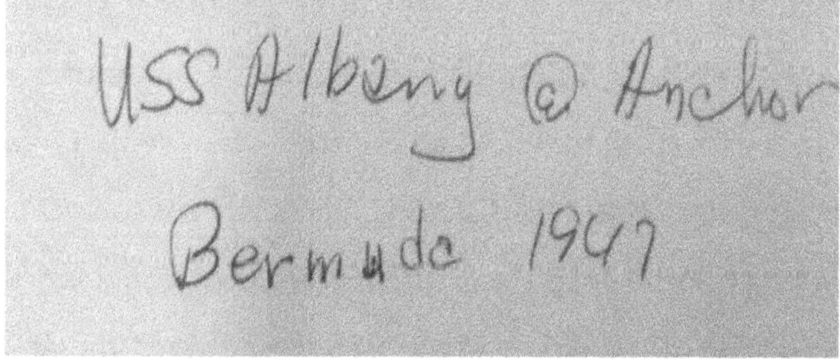

The Reason for the Navy

The reason that I picked the Navy was to stay out of the Army! I had several people from the Army in WW I that said, "Pick the Navy and if you get hit, it will be over quick, not in the field, shot full of holes where there is no one to come and help you out." So, I listened! I had no desire to go into the Army! I had four friends in High School, and of the four, two went into the Army, and two went into the Navy.

My Best Friend

My best friend went into the Navy, and he chose to stay in and made a career of it. He would go to the schools and recruit students to join the Navy. He did that well enough to become an Officer. He worked his way through a lot of years to become Lt. Commander. Then he went home one day and that was it. His wife and 3 kids were gone. As it turned out, Jim was more married to the Navy than to his family. His way of seeing it was the Navy came first and his family second. I could never do that. My family was first and has always been first in my life. My job was important as it allowed me to care for my family, but the job was always second place.

My Discharge

The time came, which was the day before I got to be 21, that the Navy had to discharge me. So, about 2-3 months before that discharge of my hitch, they worked to try to keep me in. I had enlisted when I was 17 as a minority. The rules required that I be discharged before I got to be 21. So, they HAD to discharge me. Once I was discharged, they could work to try to get me to re-enlist. They did need men, as the Korean War was coming along, but they could NOT ask me to re-enlist without first discharging me.

A Loop Hole

I was NOT re-enlisting. Several people in my unit were recalled at that time, but I was not recalled. They signed up for 2 years but were NOT minority, and they could not get 'discharged' and could not get released as they were 'extended'.

Oddly, I had been ready to enlist for a 2-year hitch, but before I did enlist in the Navy, the Navy came up with a rule that allowed men 17 to enroll as 'minority' and because I took advantage of that rule, I did not have to go back! I thank the Lord for that rule that came just as I signed up!

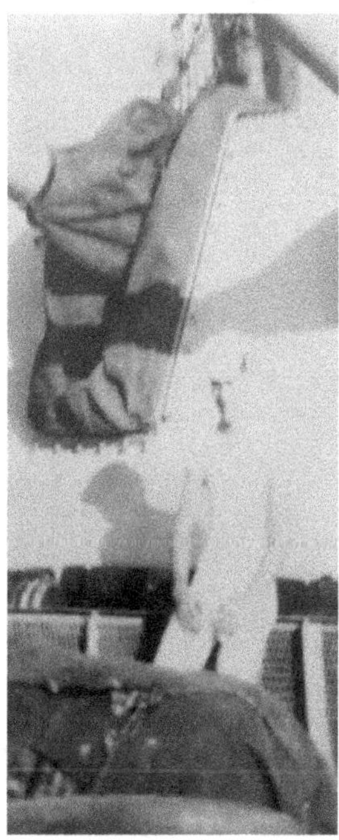

Chapter 8 - My Navy Days

Down Time

There were times when we did get to have some 'down time' when I was in the Navy. There were about 4-8 of us that would get together to play double P-knuckle cards. We would use two decks of cards. That kept the game going for a long time! The stack of cards was 9" high!

There was no money, and we had to work to find times that the players could play when they were off duty. We would sit and gather around the wooden part of the deck to play.

USS Fargo @ Anchor
off Naples 1947
Taken from Motor Launch
Enroute Naples to be
Confirmed by Bishop of Naples

Ports of the World

I was on two ships: The USS Albany and The USS Fargo. The ships were sailing in the Atlantic Ocean and Mediterranean Sea. We did land in various ports, and there were opportunities to go ashore to see places which were actually 'pretty bad'.

Naples

I did go ashore in Naples. There was not a lot 'to do' when you were off ship but go to bars so I rarely went. My Catholic confirmation happened in Naples, to enable me to be able to marry Terry as a Catholic.

France

I went ashore in France to get some expensive perfume for Terry. She never opened that bottle of expensive perfume, and it is still upstairs.

Other Countries Visited

The other countries I visited were Italy and Malta. I was on the northern island of Malta. We passed by at the end of the war and there was not much left of it! It had been bombed beyond recognition by WWII planes.

Smoking

One of the benefits of being in the service was they gave you free cigarettes. I started smoking because they were FREE! I had a buddy who also smoked, and one day I noticed he was not smoking. So, I asked my buddy why he wasn't smoking. He told he had quit for 'Lent'. Then I decided I, too, would quit for Lent. After Lent, I went back to smoking but the cigarettes made me very sick. So, I decided I would start smoking a pipe! I did that for a month after Lent, so that I COULD go back to smoking the cigarettes without having them make me sick!

Lent

For 3 years, every Lent, I would give up smoking. Then after Lent, I would smoke the pipe, and then go back to smoking the cigarettes. Then, on the fourth year, I thought "What am I doing?" Do I really want to 'like' smoking so much that I need to continue to do this? Then, I just gave up smoking after Lent, and never went back to the pipe or the cigarettes.

The Letters

Terry and I wrote letters to each other while I was in the Navy. Sometimes **Ship A** would be travelling through when they would be close to **Ship B** and they would have a bag of mail for our ship, and you would get the mail which was then 'old'.

The Late Mail

Terry would ask me to write more, but even when I wrote her five letters in a row, those letters would sometimes just sit in the mailbox of the ship and then she would receive those five letters all at the same time. So, I wrote, but the letters did not get off the ship until another ship arrived to take them.

The White Glove

We had a Lt. Commander who was noted for being a 'real horse's neck' and if there was even a 'speck' of dust he was going to find it! My responsibility to my main unit as 'main operator' was to have my crew make the place so clean that his 'white glove' would not be able to pick up even one speck of dust in the room. It was a challenge to clean the BXX Shield cable which was 3 cords of electrical wires with each one insulated by plastic and twisted inside a shield with a spring with wires in it. These were very difficult to clean and needed to be cleaned.

Everyone pushed through to 'touch clean' so the Commander in his white uniform who was looking for a speck of dust with his 'white glove' would not find one. He arrived and did his very best with his white glove. We all waited, holding our breath. When he got ready to go out, he said, "It looks like you did a good job, no dust anywhere, first class Ace job, I will give you a high mark." Now, there was a cabinet next to the door and he reached up to touch the top of that cabinet. He could reach the top because he was 6 feet tall. He took a swipe of the top of that cabinet, and it looked like he had been in a coal mine! I laughed so hard! He said,

"Well Bryer, if I were you, I would laugh too!" I said, "That must have been missed by everyone up to now!" I said, "I missed it because I'm stupid!" Commander Harold did not laugh. I said, "Yes, I laughed! I couldn't help myself! We cleaned and cleaned and this cabinet, the biggest thing in the place, was not cleaned!" He replied, "So do it now!" I replied, "Yes Sir, we will clean it! I cannot do anything about your glove, and I would give you a set of white gloves, but I don't have them, but I can send them to the cleaners for you!" He cracked a big smile, "Well, Bryer, I expect you will clean it immediately." The marine with him turned pale but did not laugh. The Commander replied, "In as much as there has been many years since this has been cleaned, I am not going to hold this against you. and you have done a good job, and I will give you a high mark." I cannot remember a time when I have laughed as hard as I laughed that day!

Chapter 9 – Our Family Begins

The 'Kids' Arrive

When Terry became sick most mornings, we knew we would have our first arrival.

Charlotte

Charlotte arrived in 1950. There was little question about what name she would be named. My father's first name was Charles, and the female equivalent of that name is "Charlotte'. In 1950, at that time, the name Charlotte for a girl was **NOT** trendy, or even used.

Our Child in Heaven

Terry, then, had a miscarriage between Charlotte and Catherine, so our family has a child in heaven waiting for us. This was tough, but Terry got pregnant again!

Catherine – "Cathy"

The doctor put Terry in the hospital early to make sure there was no danger of another miscarriage. She got two shots in her butt every day to ensure a safe delivery. It is funny 'now', but it wasn't very funny back then! Terry ended up not have any problem having Cathy! Cathy arrived in 1953. Now we had two girls!

Pamela - "Pam"

Pam was born in 1956.

Now we had three girls -all in a row! Charlotte and Cathy and Pam!

Steven – "Steve"

The next pregnancy we fully expected another girl, but much to our surprise, we had a boy: Steven. Steve was born in 1958.

The three girls treated Steve like he was a 'doll' wheeling him up and down High Street in a baby stroller. One day, a woman asked to see the baby doll. Steve sat up in the stroller and announced, "I'm **NOT** a doll!" The woman stepped back and exclaimed, 'It's not a doll! It's a child!" That surprised the 'heck' out of her!

The Dragon Trees

All of the kids loved to play at the camp site. There was a willow tree that was just 'made' for climbing. The trunk was wide and flat, and allowed them to run right up the limb on it. There were other limbs that stuck out over the lawn about ten feet. Then, there were other trees in the pasture behind the camp on the Lapan Bay side that grew over the water that looked like 'dragons' and they loved to climb and play on them too!

Our Home

Terry was an 'at home' Mom at a time when that was just beginning to be 'not usual'. The kitchen had steam heat and there was a radiator that warmed that kitchen and anyone who got near it.

Making Donuts

When the girls would go to school, Steve used to help Terry make the donuts. By the time he was 3 years old, he could push a chair up to the counter, and climb up onto the counter, which was quite wide, and pull out all of the ingredients, in the order they were used, and then put the ingredients together to make the donuts. We did not let him put the donuts into the oil, but he did everything else.

Steve's Secret Surprise

When Steve went to New Hampshire College, a group of the kids there starting chatting, and one of them said they would love to have a 'donut'. Steve told them he could make them and would do that if they would get the ingredients. Those students got the ingredients and Steve made them donuts! Everyone was amazed that Steve knew **HOW** to make donuts!

Charlotte

Charlotte was the quiet one! When she was about two years old, Terry and I were sitting in our living room and suddenly we both became aware that Charlotte was no longer in sight. I called out to her, "Charlotte, where are you?" Her quick reply, "Me busy". We could tell she was in the bathroom. We asked again, and she replied again, "Me busy!" We could hear a strange noise that sounded like, 'bing, bing, bing'". When we investigated the bathroom, I shook my head at what we saw. Charlotte was standing up, holding herself up with one hand and using the other hand to pull the toilet tissue off the roll. She had a BIG pile of toilet tissue at her feet and the roll was almost gone. "Me Busy!" she said, as she looked at us. We explained to her that we needed the tissue on the roll! We didn't know if she understood but that was the first, and the last time, she did THAT to toilet tissue.

Charlotte married her childhood friend Jim. They both became teachers in elementary school. Charlotte continued her education to get a master's degrees. She could have continued and received a PhD, but she saw that there wasn't any more financial gain, so she continued to take courses, but did not pursue that degree.

Cathy

All my girls are talented. I remember Cathy calling me once very excited. She had an opportunity to acquire a sewing machine. She told me she was working to get it. When I got off the phone, Terry and I talked, and we decided to send her the funds so she could get it sooner. She was excited. Once she had it in her home, David created a room in their home with tables for her sewing projects. She started making hair ties and placed them onto a hula hoop that had been cut to allow her to load the hoop with the hair ties. She had many salons that sold them for her. She created a set of sunflower hair ties and sent those ties to the USA rowing team. When the competition began, we watched for the USA team on television. On their last row, they showed up with those hair ties in their blonde hair. Cathy shouted, "They're wearing my bows!" She was so excited she jumped right off the floor! "Those are my bows!" Cathy created embroidered pictures of all our houses that we lived in including the camp. David created the pattern layout for her, and she did the needlework. Recently, when I needed cushions, she came and cut foam and covered them in fabric for me. The embroidered house pictures are hung in our Lake Home now on our walls.

Traditions for Christmas

We did have some Christmas traditions and one of them was making 'caramel pudding'. We would take a can of condensed milk (not evaporated milk) and submerge it in water and boil it for 3 hours and then cool it in in the fridge. Once cool, we could open 'both ends' of the can and slide it out and cut off a slice.

The Origin of our Family Hit Recipe

My sister Millie worked at a National Life event in Montpelier, and someone brought that dish to a gathering. My sister then 'passed' that recipe onto us! We made it every Christmas!

Pam - A Surprise Gift

One year Pam came to me and asked for money to get Christmas presents downtown. At six years old, back then, we could let her go down to Main Street to shop. When she came back, she said she had picked out gifts for everyone and for us, her Mom and Dad as well, for .25 cents and .50 cents. It took everything within me not to 'cry' it was so sweet. I asked her, "How much money do you need?" She told me .75 cents. I gave her a dollar and that was one of our best Christmas's ever.

20 High Street

When Terry and I arrived in St. Albans, Vermont from Northfield, Vermont, due to my position with the Railroad, we rented a home on Elm Street next to Houghton Park and lived there for almost five years.

A friend told me of a home for sale on 20 High Street. The Realtor had

had the home on the market 10 months without any buyers. It was not the best house in the world. The conditions in the City were old too. There were only two homes that sold in the city that year, and 20 High Street would be one of them. We purchased it in 1960 or 1961 for $9,000.

Although the price was not the best, when I sought advice, I was told that purchasing the home was a good idea, so we went ahead, and become homeowners. The home had 'knob and tube' wiring. I changed what I could, but I could not change all of it.

Our 1793 -1800 House

The main part of the home was built in 1793 and the other part was added on later in the 1800's. The home had another section added onto it, but the home had original beams from the 1800's inside. The house wasn't straight like a carpenter would build it today.

The Work Needed

The Dining Room wall that went towards the Street was 2" off from the top to the bottom. The wall bowed out towards Bishop Street. I had to work to 'fill it in' to get a straight wall. I insulated and put on knotty pine boards.

The Kitchen and Dining Room wall was the original part of the house and was hard to 'add' an electrical extension because the wall had a hollow space, but that was filled with 'bricks and mortar'. This was done as an attempt to make it weather tight. The second section was all rough and had dead air space to keep the cold out, as that is what they did back then.

When I attempted to add a light on one side of the dining room, that backed up to the cellar stairs, I couldn't find a hollow space, the wall was solid boards. I was able to work around it, but it was a challenge!

Our New Home

It was soon apparent that our 20 High Street home and office location was too small to accommodate the growing business and our growing family. After changing jobs from the Railroad to State Farm, an opportunity opened for us to purchase a home located on Fairfax Road. The home came with 3 acres of land! We also purchased the office building on Fairfax Road. Once purchased the move was made.

Our New Office Building on Fairfax Road (corner of Fairfield Hill Road)

City Feed had originally built the building and they had an endless supply of lumber, so the building was well constructed. I purchased the building for $35,000. It needed a lot of work! I put another $35,000 into it to make it functional for office space.

Apartments to Offices

Our new office building was used by the Air Force to provide housing for Sergeants and above, with apartments that were rented out to them. We started with the first floor and two office rooms, but quickly realized we needed more space and moved upstairs where there were four offices.

The Veterinarians rented the ground floor and that worked well for many years. Eventually I sold the entire building to Kent & April Henderson and another one of the vets. They had a good year. That year they paid off their mortgage entirely to me.

Chapter 10 – My Railroad Position

My 17 years with the Railroad

After the Navy, I went to work for the Central Vermont Railroad, Inc. I applied for OJT training for 6 months. Sunday, April 9 was my first day on the telegrapher roster.

Telegrapher

My first five years was as a 'Telegraph Operator' sending messages to someone attached to the trains giving them information for the train.

The Train Dispatcher

Then, I took another position where I worked as a 'Train Dispatcher'. The Dispatch position paid ½ again as much as my Telegraph Operator position, so that was wonderful.

The new position contained a great deal of responsibility, and many did not want the position for 'that' very reason. Critical decisions were made 'everyday' to keep the trains moving and to make sure 'two trains' weren't on the same track headed towards each other.

Train Dispatchers told the train which cars to 'pick up' and 'drop off' at any particular station. "That" is why the Train Dispatchers had the highest paying job! We had to 'gear our lives' around the job.

Work Orders

We used 'work orders' which were written to 'tell' what trains to meet, and to 'direct' trains to be 'work trains'. Those 'work trains' were given 'favor', as 'those' were the ones that we worked hard on. We worked as fast as we could to minimize any delays.

Sometimes someone would want to get information to a train. Then, we would write a 'train order sheet' and that 'sheet' had to be handed to the train as it went by.

The Yellow Line

I would go and stand as close to the 'yellow line' as I could and hold my arm up, holding onto the train order. Then the Brakeman on the train would rush out and pick it 'up' out of my hand as the train went by.

Dangerous work

Most of the time the Brakeman caught the 'order', but I remember one time when "Draper" missed it! He joked and teased me and told me I had a 'soft job'. I said, "Don't' get too sassy, or I'll hold on to the order, and 'catch a Brakeman!" (Meaning: I could 'hang onto' that 'order' and possibly 'pull him' off the train with him trying to take it from me).

I was working most of the time in different stations up and down the railroad line. I would do fill in work when someone went on vacation, so I worked in lots of different locations in Vermont.

The Night Shift

I began working the night shift. I worked Midnight to 7 am, every night, with Friday and Saturday nights off. Working nights was challenging as it was hard to sleep during the day. But there was no way to get off the night shifts. Every time there seemed like there might be an opening, the procedures used would change, and less people would be needed. And there were employees with higher seniority than me, who would have the 'first chance' for the day shifts. When it became clear that I was going to be permanently doing nights, I became very anxious to leave! The opportunity for change came soon after, when a door opened for me to work as a sales agent for State Farm.

The Trains

There were trains that were NOT stopped, but we would simply raise the flag or Lantern to push them through a station. There was NO communication to the train engineer in the front of the train, it was all done through paper train orders in route at the back of the train. When in route they would open the copy order and convey the information to the engineer. The telephone was used to change a train order – that was the rule of thumb. Sometimes a Train Dispatcher would do a change order using the telegraph.

Trains moved from White River Junction to St. Albans and were put together in White River Junction. Trains also moved from St. Johnsbury and from White River Junction to South New London. To move any train, a 'train order' was needed from a Train Dispatcher.

The Train Wreck

There was a train that derailed in route that required making sure all other trains were stopped at that busy time of day and held until the tracks were cleared, and that took time.

The train that brought the crane could only travel at 10 -12 mph and that was very slow due to the weight of the crane on the train. Train Dispatchers worked to move the trains as fast as they could according to the Rule Book – but ALWAYS according to the rules!

Those Railroad Tracks

How the railroad tracks were determined is 'a story'. The Surveyors between White River Junction and St. Albans Vermont would 'know' where the railroad was going to be located and would go ahead of the railroad and purchase two sections of 10 acres each from the farmers along the route, and then resell their purchases to the railroad at a substantial profit. This was very 'crooked' but well known.

There were much better routes to get from Barre/Moretown than the route taken, because Roxbury has a very steep hill but the profit being made by the surveyors determined where the rails were laid!

The Loss of My Good Friend Vern!

My friend Vernon Church and I worked together on the Railroad. He planned to retire within a year when there was a terrible accident. The accident happened between Williston and Essex Junction. A bad thunderstorm washed out a huge ravine and the railroad track rails fell into that hole. There was no way of knowing that the tracks had fallen into that hole. The Brakeman pulled on the brakes to stop the train, and the quick jolt to stop was so great, that Vernon, who was walking between railroad cars, was flattened.

Terry and I felt the loss of our good friend deeply, and our children also felt the loss, as Vernon and his wife had children who were the same age as ours. We got together often, and they would play together. Vern had one boy and four girls. I always stopped at his camp to say hello.

Chapter 11 – State Farm

STATE FARM

Allen K. White at State Farm told me about the possibility of my being a sales agent. There were no slots open at the time but soon thereafter, one of the agents got into the 'til' and took funds inappropriately. That opened the door for me to be a sales agent.

So, at 39 years old, I left the Railroad and began my career with State Farm. This was a wonderful opportunity and a blessing to me and my family. Terry became my assistant and we created space off our dining/living area for an office. Our home became a 'business location.' The business quickly took off and I quit my job for the Railroad and did insurance sales full time.

My Goal

My goal was to help as many people as I could to be insured. State Farm insured homes as well as vehicles. There were some homes that I could not insure. Joe! My good friend Joe was one of those who had property that State Farm would just not accept to insure. These were rental properties that were older and, with tenants renting the locations, they were not good insurance bets. Joe and I remained friends even though I could not help with insuring his rental properties. Much later, when he stopped renting, I was able to provide him with insurance. We have been friends for over 65 years now! And Joe is still one of my best friends! He even shoveled out 6 feet of snow so he would be able to enter our home to turn off the alarm one winter.

Travel

State Farm would often require me to travel. One trip was to the Regional Office in New Jersey where I went to school for a week. On another trip there was a terrible storm! The cars were off the road all over the median. Rain was pouring buckets. My arms starting aching during the drive. I was gripping the steering wheel so bad, that my muscles were all tightened up. I would talk to myself and tell myself to "relax, relax, relax", but I was happy when the rain was behind me on THAT trip.

And I was very fortunate to not have had any accidents, or to have gone off the road on those trips.

The Claims

Being an agent involved dealing with claims. One claim was most distressing. A family called that had lost their home in a fire overnight. I arrived the next morning to the site. It was discouraging to see. Really 'nothing' but the foundation was left; all was just smoldering in the ashes. There was nothing left, everything was gone.

The fireman explained to me that as they pulled up, the first window blew out, and then the front windows went out and it burned to the floor. The basement walls looked 'white' to me.

As I met with the homeowner, I leaned on my car and took out my checkbook and wrote him a check right away. He was shocked. The action I took was bold, but I knew State Farm would be good for the money.

This was a family in true 'need', and this was what I did for a living: helping people deal with losses and get back on their feet as quickly as possible.

This family really needed help and I was able to give it to them right away! State Farm never questioned the claim submitted and provided even more money than what I initially gave to them.

Another Total Loss

Another total loss was a split-level home that burned down to the concrete. The only thing left on that property was a refrigerator. It was standing in the corner, but it was the only thing left on site!

State Farm Fish Tales

Most days when I worked at our State Farm office building, I would go home for lunch from Noon to 1 pm. When I would get home on most winter days, Terry would say, "Do you have to go back to work today? Can we go fishing?" She loved to ice fish. She wasn't interested in boat fishing unless she could be kept busy on the boat!

The Tricky Fish

One winter when we were ice fishing, I felt a fish and pulled up my hook only to find just a fisheye on it! We kept fishing and suddenly I had another bite. This time it was a 'fish'! When we got the fish out and looked at it, it was a fish with only 1 eye! I had caught the same fish that I had caught that had lost its eye!

My Big Find

We fished the Lake shore where our camp is located. I would go in the Spring and walk the shore looking for signs of fish. On one walk I went past our camp down about 3-4 camps and was shocked to see something large in the water. It was a 7' foot Sturgeon as big as a person that was dead on the shore. The Fish and Game came and towed it out into deeper water that year, but it was the largest fish I have ever seen!

5 Gallons of Fish!

Terry and I liked to fish with Ray and Joyce Leblanc. One day we planned to go fishing and I was to meet them at the boat. I had a client and was running about 45 minutes late. When I got there, they were all at the camp and the boat was out of the water. I wondered what was going on. Ray then told me of their most amazing experience.

He had anchored the boat about ½ mile out in 30 feet of water and Terry and Joyce had started to fish. He put the bait on the hooks for both, and would have started to fish himself, but they both started catching perch, one right after the other. He sat in the middle of the boat and took the fish off the line for them. As soon as he would get one line baited, the other would catch another perch, so he would take that off the hook and bait the hook again. This continued until they had filled that 5-gallon pail full of fish!

We both loved to fish! And we caught lots of large fish! If the fish were less than 7 inches, we would throw them back!

Chapter 12 – The Lake Camp

One of the first places Terry and I loved to go was to the Lake. Shantee Point Road was right along the water and there were very few camps on the road at that time because most of the road would be completely washed out after the Spring rains were finished. Then the road had to be patched to even be passable. There was a camp called "Merry Dawn" but that was one of the only camps on the road and is presently owned by Steve Gellis.

We would go down to what is now our 'camp' site and enjoy being on the water. There was a large 'fenced in' pasture opposite to the road where the home now sits.

The Kids Loved to Swim

Terry and I would bring the children down, and one of us would sit on a rock and watch them on the shore all the time they were in the water. We never left the children alone, ever, when they were playing in the lake. One of us, would always be there on the shore ready if any 'one' of them needed our help.

This location on Shantee Point Road became our site for getting away. I was able to lease the land. At that time, we had no funds available to put a camp up, without sacrificing things for our family.

The Chance of a Lifetime

Vernon Church, a friend of mine who was a Brakeman on the Railroad with me, told me that he had purchased the old East Swanton Station to disassemble and then put back together. That made me wonder if there might be any other stations that might be available for sale. Indeed, there was one located in Middlesex. That station was being used for storage by a lumber company. I was told that when they were through with 'it' I could purchase it. Soon after, it was available! I offered them $50 and they accepted. It was a freight house with big roller barn doors. I was able to sell the 'barn doors' with their hardware to a nearby farmer who came and disassembled them and took them.

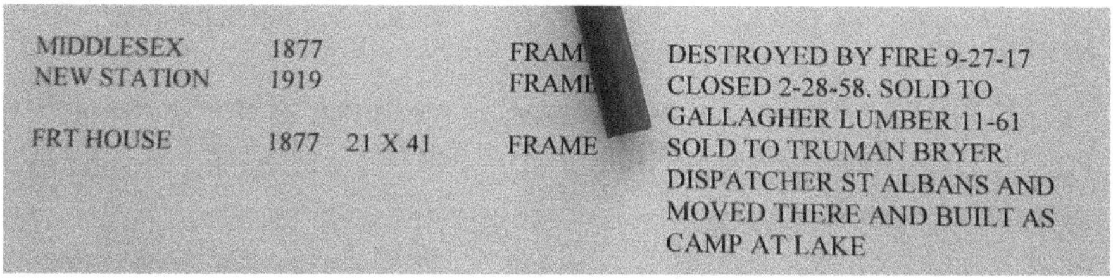

MIDDLESEX	1877		FRAME	DESTROYED BY FIRE 9-27-17
NEW STATION	1919		FRAME	CLOSED 2-28-58. SOLD TO GALLAGHER LUMBER 11-61
FRT HOUSE	1877	21 X 41	FRAME	SOLD TO TRUMAN BRYER DISPATCHER ST ALBANS AND MOVED THERE AND BUILT AS CAMP AT LAKE

The Long Work Begins

The purchase of the Station began a very long process that lasted over two years. Every Monday and Tuesday, on my days off, I would travel to Middlesex and work to take the building apart. The job was labor intensive due to having to 'label' and separate each section into piles. Some of the lumber was much larger than what I would need for the camp. That 'wood' had to be cut smaller. The floor joists were cut 4x12 and then were cut in half to 4x5 for floor joists. These were brought and cut on site. The lumber being cut also contained hidden 'spikes'. When the saw blade hit one of those, I would hear it grind. That noise would make my back lift as it typically meant a new blade was needed.

The BIG Move

Finally, the day came when the entire structure was in piles on the ground, ready to be moved. We hired a driver with a truck to pick up all the pieces of the building and deliver them to our Shantee Point Road camp location. Once that was done, it would take another two years to reconstruct the entire building, piece by piece. It took a total of five years before the inside was ready for bringing in furniture and being able to use it as a 'camp' and not just a place to come in out of the sun or cold. For two years it was covered just with tar paper.

The Barn

Then, I finally found a barn with barn boards and purchased that from a farmer. The U.S. Government bought the farm area where the barn was located and had moved a small building to a different location but left the main barn. I was able to purchase it for $50 and then 'that' had to be disassembled. Another farmer was interested in the metal roof, and he came and removed the roof and left the barn boards, which was the only thing I really wanted.

The Farmer's Gift

The farmer was so pleased to get the roofing, that he loaded the barn boards onto his pickup truck and delivered them to the camp site. I was able to add the barn boards over the tar paper on the camp. Then, I added insulation to the ceiling and sheetrock to the walls.

The Gift of Friendship!

Through the years, I would work for others, and as I helped them in similar fashion, they would exchange their labor and come and help me. Vern allowed me to use his tools whenever I needed them. This was a **HUGE** help to me. I had the drive and ambition, and he had the tools!

When lumber needed to be cut and trimmed, he would call me, and we would spend hours together doing projects.

The Seasons

In the winter we would bundle up and go 'ice fishing'. In the spring the kids would climb trees and sit on the limbs. Summer was full of swimming, and outdoor fires. Fall was full of inside and outside games in our new summer camp.

The Flood

One spring we had lots of rain and the high water made it possible for the kids to paddle a boat around the camp. Our camp was high enough to escape being flooded.

The Camp Upgrade

In 1996 we had the opportunity to have a home built on the site. That would require removal of the Railroad station camp. I decided rather than just remove the camp, I would let people know that we were willing to sell the camp for $1000 with a stipulation that whoever purchased it would have to move it! Amazingly, we had a purchaser right away on Shantee Point Road. The lady that bought it placed our railroad station camp going east to west of the building already there, and tied the roofs together. The camp is painted red now and we pass it every day coming and going to our new home.

The new home was built and received an award for innovative design. It was featured on the cover of an Architectural magazine. Once it was finished, people started to show up at our door wanting to come and see inside. We allowed people to come and tour our home for quite a while. It was very amazing.

Camp rebuilt from Middlesex station – (Note: Road is on located on waterfront)

Camp relocated to new location

New home with road moved to new location behind the home.

Chapter 13 – The New Road

The road to the camp went along the waterfront, between the camp and the Lake. Several attempts were made to try and make a road that would go 'behind' the camps but each one failed.

The Key Player

One year, I decided to talk with my fellow neighbor Joe about making another attempt to possibly move the road. Joe was not encouraging. "We have tried several times and it is to no avail. You would be wasting your time! It cannot be done." My reply, "Well, let me give it one more try!" Joe was not impressed and predicted that much money would be wasted plus a lot of my time. However, I knew our family had a key player that might enable the project to move forward: Peter Cross!

Peter's Expertise

Peter knew other environmental engineers who were able to do the surveying required to identify the 'wetlands' and to present their findings to the powers that be. Peter offered his help with providing surveying without cost and presented the Board 'in charge' with a proposed road that went the entire length from the initial curve to the end.

The Opposition

Unfortunately, there was opposition from just 'one' of the landowners who stalled. He said, "I need to have time to talk to my renters!"

His intent was never to talk to 'his renters' but simply to 'stop' the project from happening. When it became apparent it would be impossible to get him to change his mind, an alternative was made.

Getting Around the Obstacle

One lot would be purchased that would allow for the road to take a sharp LEFT turn once over the small creek and then turn RIGHT and meander behind the waterfront properties.

Eight homeowners benefited when the day arrived that the plans were approved. And it was with a BIG smile that I went to visit Joe with the news to my friend Joe, 'It's been approved!" Sadly, the chance for the other homeowners to have a road located behind rather than along the waterfront, would now cost much more, and is very unlikely to occur.

Life Lessons

Life offers opportunities to us when 'doors open' and amazing things can happen when everyone pulls together. It took three years for the plans to be approved, but the benefit for those who worked together is great! We do not have 'dust' and 'cars' moving in front of our homes. We no longer have to look both ways before reaching the water, and we have the most amazing views of the Lake from our new front lawn areas!

"Thank you, Peter, for all you did to take the dream – to our new reality!"

Chapter 14 – Miscellaneous Memories

My Boats

I had a 16–18-foot green boat. It was a fishing boat, not a yacht. Then, I went to a 24 foot pontoon boat that was very stable and could hold 15-16 people. It had a pilot seat and a windshield.

It was all I could do to get Terry on any boat. She didn't know how to swim, so she didn't favor being on any boat. She would get on a boat to go fishing but that was it.

Our Perfect Fishing Spot

We had a sweet fishing spot that was about ½ mile out. Ray and Joyce came up to go fishing a lot and we got some beautiful perch from that location. We would go and line the boat up the St. Albans Radar Base dome and then 'just so' we could see past Woods Island. We were in about 30 feet of water on the spot, and we got fish there every time we went out that season. That year we would throw anything that was 7-8" back and would only keep the perch that were 9-11" and we had all you could eat!

I did the cleaning with Ray. We never asked Terry or Joyce to clean the fish!

Ice Fishing

Ray and I went out on the ice to go ice fishing one winter. Ray insisted we keep going further out. I could hear the ice going 'crackle, crackle,

crackle" and I finally told him "We are far enough out!" So, we stopped and dug a trench about 4'x 4' Ray wanted to put down a line as soon as he could. As soon as he got a line in the water, he started catching as quick as he could put the line in and pull it out! The perch were biting like crazy that day!

The Hollow Trees

There was a big Weeping Willow tree that was 'hollow' inside on the road opposite the driveway entrance located next to the Green Boat Trailer on the left side of road. You could only see that it was 'hollow' from its back side. That tree must have been created when God created the earth. The tree was very large!

The other 'hollow' tree was on the side of our driveway, and we didn't even know that it was hollow inside. We had a swing on it, and we had to shorten the swing because the swing was hitting the ground. We never thought to check 'why' the swing was hitting the ground. Once it was sawed into, we could see it was totally hollow inside and there was hardly anything holding it up! There could have been a big problem with the tree falling and hurting someone, but that did not happen, thank the Lord!

Raymond LeBlanc

I really enjoyed visiting with Raymond LeBlanc. We used to have them here almost every weekend. They would come and stay in a motor home or in a tent or just come for the day! They live right in South Burlington,

Vermont. Our families were close for many, many years.

Lou Gordon

I was blessed to have a broker named Lou Gordon. He was interested in his clients and was in the minority because most brokers are not interested in their clients. He had my interests as high as his own and put my interests first.

Hippopotamus

I remember my Mom telling me how to pronounce Hippopotamus: "hipp hop a tom a mus' !

Our Beach

Our beach is very clean. We had a spell a few years ago when we had algae the came to the shore. I would go down with a rake and pick it up out of the water and place it in piles 5'x 2' on the shore. It weighed a 'ton' when I was taking it out of the water, but once it drained out and the sun dried it, it was very easy to move. We used it for compost on our garden!

Electricity for the Shore

I installed electricity on a tree on the beach for the boat. The smaller the # of the wire the larger the power. I used #2 and #4 wire to make sure we have enough power.

Steve's Tree House

When Steve was a young boy, he made a tree house out of the three trees on the shore. The shore trees were the size of my 'arms' at the time, and he was able to put wooden boards between them in the middle. The kids spent hours playing in that tree house. Those same trees now are huge!

How Time Flies!

I remember when my grandparents used to comment how fast time flies, and I never understood what they meant, but I sure understand 'now'!

Campfires

We used to build 'camp' fires with our friends Roy and Joyce and their families that would come, and we would sit around the fire pit. The fire pit was made from flat rocks to fill up the bottom and I used the rocks that the waves brought in for the outer circle. Each year the waves would move all the stones in the fire pit, and a new pit would have to be made, but we had a lot of fun building those fire pits back then!

The Seagulls

We used to have a lot of sea gulls. There would be all over the place, but I don't see many of them now. Where did they all go? It's quite a mystery!

Trueman Humor

Recently Peter came down with a chair to visit me on the front lawn.

Trueman: "Want to lease a spot to sit?"

Peter: 'Okay, I can lease a spot!"

Trueman: "You will be charged according to how much you enjoy it!"

Peter: "Okay, I will be sure to not enjoy it too much!"

Charlotte: Thinking about something you want to talk about?

Jim: I think I can hear 'wind' whistling through 'somewhere' your ears?

Trueman: Maybe. .

Pam: "Like my new coat Dad?"

Trueman: "You have a 'coat of many colors' just like in the Bible!

Trueman: She's a good egg: slightly cracked but good!

Visit of Ray & Joyce LeBlanc

Ray: How are you?

Trueman: Mean and grumpy as usual!

Trueman: Ray was a State Farm Agent who was 10 years younger than me!

Ray: I was the best State Farm Agent in Vermont! One time we stayed on the top floor of the Pegasus for our 50th Anniversary!

Joyce: Well, there was more to it than that!

Ray: Our kids were going to stay at a Motor Home.

Trueman: We were just talking about Skating here!

Ray: Shall I hang up my coat?!

Trueman: Give it to me and I'll hang it up and go through your wallet! LOL

Ray: Always genuine! He says: Let's go out to dinner, Let's split it! Give me your card and I'll give the waitress both cards to split it. A month later, both charges were on my card!

Joyce: And they were lobster dinners too!

Ray: It was Coupies Motel – or 'Crappy's Motel!

Joyce: We had made a reservation for 'late arrival' but when we arrived late, they had given rooms to somebody else!

Ray: We went to restaurant to figure out what to do, and they suggested cabins with 2 rooms.

Joyce: Ray and I went to bed and immediately fell into the "center" of the mattress. Trueman and Terry had a bed with a misplaced bed spring and didn't dare move all night – he didn't want to be castrated! They had a sign for going to the bathroom and they had these paper slippers for you to wear. At least we were not out on the street! Then, a year goes by, and I get a 'slipper' in the mail with "Happy Birthday" written on it from Trueman!

Ray: That's not whole story! Trueman, then sent me a bill in the mail for the whole thing!

Joyce: We did a lot of stuff here. Trueman cleared off an area and put in power so we could park our motor home and bring it to camp here. Then, he put a 'stuffed skunk' on the steps and stood back and waited and watched, as I saw 'it' and started backing up!

Trueman: I wasn't afraid! I was going to go and hit it with a stick to get it out of there! LOL

Ray: We visited here one year and set off fireworks and one went off so fast that it went another way and under Bob Noel's chair! Boy did he jump! (Another State Farm Agent).

Joyce: Trueman brought truckloads of 'sand' so that we could play in the water on the shore, so it wouldn't be rocky! He even took time to pick the rocks out of the path so we could walk down to the sand.

Charlotte: I remember Ray playing horseshoes.

Cathy: I think of Peter Cross's grandfather who loved playing horseshoes and being around younger people.

Ray: Trueman babbles a lot! If you have a question, ask me! I'll give you the truth – talk to ME, I'll give you the truth!

Joyce: I had double surgery at Dartmouth 13 years ago. I fit all the criteria and in recovery I could not favor one side over the other, I had to balance myself and that helped my recovery.

Trueman: After getting with Ray, you weren't 'balanced' at all! LOL

Joyce: We love coming to visit here – still do!

Chapter 15 -Letter from Pam

Christmas 2009

Mom & Dad,
I thought it might be fun for me to take a trip down memory lane from my childhood. These are just a few of the great memories you helped to create for me:

1. Our trip to Story town.
2. Sitting on the silver kitchen radiator on a cold winter day.
3. Loading into the car on Christmas Eve to drive around looking at all the Christmas lights.
4. Having you sitting on the beach at camp for hours on end watching all four of us swimming. I would yell, "Watch me!" as I stood on my hands under water!
5. The cardboard fireplace Dad set up every Christmas, and your explanations on how Santa came down the chimney.
6. Picking 'tiny' wild strawberries at camp for Mom to make Strawberry short cake.
7. Mom dressing us up every Easter in cute dresses and hats for church. "Don't forget the Easter Baskets!"
8. You sitting on the shore watching us stand under water on our heads.
9. Mom and Steve making homemade donuts.
10. Watching "The Wonderful World of Disney".
11. Mrs. Kitchell, the Avon lady, stopping by the house to show Mom the new products. I loved the little white sample lip sticks she brought for Mom.
12. Fishing with Dad on the Lake.

13. Taking the train to Montpelier to stay with Meme and Pepe.
14. Walking down to the railroad with Mom, Cathy, and Charlotte and Steve to bring Dad his dinner in the picnic basket.
15. Carmel pudding at Christmas.
16. Tuna, croquettes and galletes (fried dough bread) with maple syrup on Wednesdays during Lent.
17. My 8th grade Birthday dinner when Mom and Dad gave me a big radio.
18. Playing in the old willow tree at camp – we spent time in that tree!
19. Making "Chatee" cakes.
20. Going to the Lake with Nana and Bope to go fishing.
21. Riding home from Salem, NY with "Cocoa" - my 1-week-old kitten.
22. Being an 'angel' at May Ceremony at St. Mary's Church.
23. Mom always being home when I got home from school.
24. Dad always having a 'project' in the house to work on.
25. Birthday party in the dining room with my friends. I had a pink and black dress and a pink tiara.
26. The big box of homemade 'ribbon candy' from Mr. & Mrs. Costes.
27. Drives up through Smugglers Notch to the Trapp Family Lodge.
28. Rowing the rowboat around the camp one Spring when the water was really high. At the time we thought that was so cool. What did we know!?

29. Going up and over the big hill at Meme and Pepe's house. Meme told us there was a bull up there and we should not go there!
30. Shoveling snow on High Street. It seemed like the snowbanks were mountains.
31. Playing in the leaves in the fall – all the leaves of the neighborhood seemed to blow into our yard. We would make huge piles and jump into them!
32. Carving very cool pumpkin faces.
33. Sitting around the bar table at camp and eating BBQ Chicken cooked on charcoal.
34. Horseshoe games at camp.
35. Christmas parties when Santa came on a dog sled pulled behind a snowmobile.
36. Dad selling "State Farm Insurance" out of the High Street house. Mom being his secretary.
37. The Christmas Party at the American Legion on Kingman Street with live music.
38. Playing croquet on the lawn at camp.
39. Playing Monopoly as a family in the dining room on High Street.

Thank you for all the sacrifices you made for your family.

Thank you for all the love you have given.

Thank you for being my Mom & Dad!

I love you!

Pamela Jean Bryer Cross

Chapter 16 -Trueman Q&A -Terry's Memories

Who was President when you were born? Calvin Coolidge, from Plymouth, VT.

Who was your favorite President? John F. Kennedy – he was popular and was killed.

Did you ever meet a famous person? Terry and I met Vanna White's Dad. He took us into his realtor's office to show us things and he was really a great guy. He took time to show us pictures of Vanna, where she lived, and it was great!

What about Valentine's? I started getting roses for Terry after we were married and continue to get them even now on Valentine's Day in her memory.

Did you have a secret hide-away place growing up? We had a 'Club for members only" out in a field.

What was the best pet you had? We had a family dog called "Prince" who was an Indian Terrier, and he was too fat! Polly the Parrot was the best pet, and Cocoa the cat!

How did you spend your Saturdays? I was in the Boy Scouts, and we had Boy Scout meetings from 7-9 pm weekdays in Northfield. There was a siren that blew at 9 pm and that was for all kids to get off the streets unless you had a written permit from your parents in your pocket! We were out at night but at the siren we had to walk or peddle home!
We went on picnics a lot.

Did you ever go to a circus? The circus came to Randolph, and they had animals. They would use elephants to hold a wooden hammer and pound the posts of the tents into the ground. We would watch from a distance. There were also two poles and a trapeze wire.

What games did you play? We played cards, and the game 'Monopoly" that game made you think, and you had to work to get ahead of that game, and "Checkers', and marbles – I had a lot of 'allies' which are glass marbles. I never played 'Dominos' I never got the hang of that game!

How did you learn to swim? I taught myself! I did a dog paddle and then went from there. In boot camp in basic training there was a swimming pool with a 30-foot platform. When they asked if anyone was afraid to jump off, I stuck my hand up and I got to go first! I swam under water and came up and was called 'wise guy' and told "You get up here!" We did go swimming in river holes. We would go upriver and find a spot and get wet on a hot day.

What radio programs did you listen to? We could listen to "The Lone Ranger" on the radio. There was no Television back then.

What chores did you have growing up? My sister did the dishes, and I was younger so I didn't do many chores when I was younger, but I did have to clean the filter bags of the cleaning fluid for my Dad's Dry Cleaning Plant when I got older. My Dad had bags of charcoal and it was a dirty job! There was a lot of dust, and it was an 'icky thing" to have to do.

Did you go to the dentist? I had two teeth out without Novocain and that alienated me towards dentists! I did lose a tooth! And we had a "tooth fairy" so I got a few cents for a tooth!

What was your first job? I worked at a cheese factory in Northfield, and they made cheese. We got to help ourselves to some of it. There were several steps to it, and I was paid a man's wage.

What holidays did you enjoy? I liked Christmas and New Year's! By High School there was 'Armistice Day" in November at the end of WWII and we got a whole day off for that! On Memorial Day there was a parade in Northfield and my Dad walked in the parade for the American Legend every year carrying the American Flag. It was very special to see my Dad in a uniform. We had 'Easter Egg Hunts" as little children. Later Terry would get dressed up on Easter and would dress up the kids for Easter for when we went to Easter Sunday church. During Halloween we would go and do 'good things'. One trick some kids would play was to move the stairs away from a house. There were 5 or 6 of us that would go around and fix that and put the stairs back. Once we got hollered at and we told them we were putting the stairs 'back' not taking them away! As a Boy Scout we did 'good things'. I did have a slingshot made from a tree branch that was divided like a fork. I used rubber bands and that made it very powerful. The Drug Store sold the rubber bands. I could purchase 'beans' for ten cents and I would take a handful of the beans and we would walk by kids and when a kid would shoot a pea through a straw at me, I would turn around with my sling shot and toss the beans at them and also at the side of a house with beans, and they would turn around to see what was making that noise! That was a lot of fun to do that did not create any problem.

Did you ever get bite by a dog? No, but there was a person that had a nasty dog. I used a telephone in my Dad's shop and called the women up and told her, "I will not deliver papers anymore unless the dog is inside. From 3- 3:30 pm I will deliver; if your dog is outside then I will NOT deliver it." She told me I was the first to complain, but I told her, "That is not true - many kids are scared of your dog!"

What do you remember about your Mom? My Mom had a good heart. She remembered special days, and birthdays and made cakes and we would get to blow out the candles. She worked and worked.

What do you remember about your Dad? My Dad knew a lot about the woods from hunting. He knew animal tracks and how to move through the woods. He grew up in Maine and it was 'need to know up there'!

What memory stands out for you growing up? During WWII when things had to be rationed. Meat, food, butter, sugar, and gasoline, all were rationed. We had air raid drills at school and we all had to get under our desks during the drills. If you could buy from a farmer, you could get around some of the restrictions.

What is the best vacation you recall? At Lake Morey. We had a leaky rowboat, but we went out on the Lake and caught perch! Every 15-20 minutes we had to bail it out and start over again always bailing it out. When I was an agent for State Farm, I qualified for a trip to Hawaii that was great. I also qualified for the State Farm high-end trips to both France and Paris! I had to dig in and produce new business for those! But they were great vacations!

Did you ever climb a mountain? When I was in the Boy Scouts, we did climb mountains. Mount Elmore Mountain on the Lake. We would hike up halfway one afternoon, make camp and have supper and sleep. In the morning we had to get up, have breakfast and climb to the top, and then go back down. Then we would have to wait for next year to do it again!

Did your Mom have a favorite remedy for when you were sick? Yes, castor oil! It was just horrible – and she made me take a teaspoon full!

What is your best talent? Telling lies! LOL! No, telling jokes! I'm a real comedian!

Did you ever get lost in the woods? Never. I grew up in the woods. My Dad would take me with him to the woods when I could barely walk. He was very good at tracking 'things' and he always had a compass. You could not get him lost!

Did you sing songs? We did sing songs. My Dad would pack the whole family in the car and go for a long ride. My Dad could sing!

What was your bedroom like growing up? I shared a bedroom with my brother! We had posters on the walls. My brother had toys and he took a stuffed teddy bear to bed.

Did you ever take a toy apart? Never! Toys were hard to come by, so I didn't want to destroy any of them!

Did you go Roller Skating? I was good at roller skating. There were skates that had metal wheels that you could use on pavement, and they were my sisters, and I used them when she wasn't around. You could go and roller skate inside a big roller-skating arena for .25 cents.

How did you learn to shave? I taught myself to shave. If I pressed down too hard, I could take a nip out of myself. It was pretty hard to learn to shave, and hard to hide a 'nick' too!

Did you have a hero? Superman! The Flash! I had several comic book heroes! They were hard to live up to though!

How have telephones changed? I will never forget the first time I tried to use a telephone. I stood in front and turned the crank and told the operator, "I want to talk to my mother!" She replied, "Mother? Can you tell me who your mother is?" They could figure it out.

Later Cathy and Charlotte worked for the Telephone Company. One winter we had a blizzard that plugged every Street and Road in St. Albans. Cars could not go anywhere. The snowfall was more than the Village equipment could handle! Cathy and Charlotte walked the distance to the telephone office. The Telephone Company needed people to work. And they learned how to connect people by dispatch when they called. Cathy was a freshman in High School, and Charlotte was a Senior and the older taught the younger one. They both walked up to the Telephone Company with their butts in the snow to get to work that day, and that put them in good stead! They were very capable to do the switchboard work.

What about going to school do you remember when you were young? I wanted to go to school, but I didn't like it after I got there! The teacher could make or break a kid's desire to learn! I had to walk about a half mile to school. We were in one room all day long. You had to hold up your hand to go to the bathroom and then you had to come right back within a reasonable time. There were report cards that had to be signed every six weeks. You were lucky to have a pair of sneakers to wear. There was always somebody who wanted to come down on someone weaker. I did break up a fight once! We could go outside for recess, depending on the weather, and we had a good size yard that had basketball hoops on two ends and a teeter-totter board with four boards on it. My sister skipped 8th grade. She did the work at the teacher's house who lived across the street. She worked for six weeks and took the final exam and skipped 8th grade. I kissed Leah! Leah had long red hair. My Dad liked Leah's family and called her 'carrot top'. Leah graduated from High School. Later in life, I met her sister who was 2-3 years younger, and she told me that Leah was sick and in a facility. I thought that was very sad! I went to Northfield Grade School, and Northfield High School. We had a Basketball team, and the girls would lead the cheering for the team!

What did you wear to school? My Mom made some of my clothes and my father made a winter overcoat for me. He had to work altering clothes for draftee's when needed, so he knew how to alter clothes. He took what he could get from a U.S. Navy overcoat and made it smaller for me to wear. The coat was not fancy, but it was warm!

Did you ever have a school cancelation of classes? We did have a snowstorm that canceled school for 23 days. Some roads had to have a tractor to push out the snow, and a lot of roads did not get done. We had sleighs pulled by horses that were used during the winter months. We made snowmen and snow forts!

What teacher did you dislike? Vesta Lyon – She was a horrible person. Sneaky! One time she left us in the 8th grade classroom and came back in on 'tip toe', sneaking in the back door until she had marked those that were acting up and then she would stand them across the front of the room. She had a 12" ruler not too thick. Once the students lined up there, she would put the smaller ruler away and take out a thick ruler and then she would strike their hand with it. She would also get a rubber hose from the janitor's room and whack the student's backside with that hose again and again.

Who was the smartest kid in school? Me! LOL! No! There were some kids with better marks than me.

What about your High School do you remember? I had 2 principals in high school. The first year Jack Erickson and another guy. One day I went home for lunch. And that day when I got back to school, I found that my 'desk' had been placed outside on the fire escape by 4-5 seniors. So, I just went out to get my books, and then when I tried to go back through the window, someone had closed that window and locked it. So, I just went and sat down and started

to do my work at my desk on that fire escape! Mr. Butler came and asked, "Trueman, what are you doing?" I replied, "I came and found my desk outside, so I came out to get my books, and *'somehow'* the window got locked and I could not get back into the classroom, so I am sitting here doing my work."
Mr. Butler said, "I don't know what is going on here." Before I could say "Jack Robinson" my desk was back inside.

Did you ever go to concerts? The Town of Northfield had a band and one night a week in the summer we would go to hear them play at the Town Common. There was a large park in the shape of a semi-circle and the cars would park around that circle. And we would sit in the cars and listen to the band and then blow the horn when a tune the liked would be played. There was a 'Goodie Store' that I would go to and would carry a bag around with two kinds of popcorn: cheese and regular. Some who could afford it would go for the cheese and there were smaller and larger sizes. I got paid .01 cent a bag whichever it was!

Did you ever have a bat in the house? We had a bat in the lake house. We came in, and all of a sudden, the bat was in the top area. We opened both ends of the house and it flew out! We always had a cat, but I never saw a mouse!

Did you get an allowance? No. We had to earn money. I did odd dirty jobs all summer for about .25 cents per job.

Did you ever pick apples? We picked apples that were wild! Years ago, about a mile from our house, there was a farm which no longer is in existence, and which has been out of farm service for years. There were only the slate foundations left and whatever apple trees that had been planted years and years ago. We would walk to that farm location and pick the apples from those trees. We would take a knapsack and fill it full of apples, and then go home and dump them out and go back and get more. My Mom would make apple puree and apple jelly with extra sugar and some applesauce. But the jelly was hard to come by, because during the war sugar was rationed and hard to come by.

How did you propose to Mom? I asked her to marry me and gave her a ring and she was very happy and so was I! We got married at St. Augustine's Church in Montpelier, VT on October 9, 1948. My Best man was Ken Harpell who was my Navy friend. We went to Boston for our honeymoon, or close to Boston, because Ken Harpell lived outside of Boston.
My only regret with Terry was that we did not have more time together! We had four children:
Charlotte Bryer Arkinson
Catherine Bryer Woelfel
Pamela Bryer Cross
Steven Michael Bryer
We picked these names for each of them because Terry and I just liked the names!

Were there other gatherings for your family? We had anniversaries for Mémé and Pépé Gaboriault their 50th, and for Terry and me, and our own 50th and 60th wedding anniversaries!

What was Christmas like? We chopped down a tree by going to a farmer and asking if we could have one from the woods and most of the time, they would let us cut one down. We strung popcorn on a string and would color the popcorn with food coloring. We had stockings stuffed with oranges, popcorn, apples, and a small bag of something special. We went to church to celebrate the birth of Jesus and I went to Sunday School.

Do you have some good advice for us? Follow the 10! (The Ten Commandments!): Love God, others, tell the truth, don't steal, etc. Have faith in Jesus, Believe. Receive! And invest in a bank!

TRUEMAN's LIKES and DISLIKES

DISLIKES:
Avocado
Mexican Food
Burnt Cabbage

LIKES
Molasses Cookies
Fish

Steak
Eggs
Fresh Corn on the Cob
Seafood
Vermont Maple Cremee
Anything with Maple Syrup
Poached Eggs on Toast
Sauteed Veggies
The "Zom Hee' Chinese Restaurant on the West Coast of Florida

BEST VACATION: "Don't have far to go! Right here on the Lake before the house existed!

FAVORITE COLOR: Blue

FAVORITE DAUGHTER: Don't make me pick! All of them!! Don't make me pick!"

BEST COOK: "I am!"

FAVORITE ACTIVITIES: "Talking, Cooking! Fishing!'

FAVORITE RESTAURANT: "The Bryer Table -Every time!"

FAVORITE MOVIES: Westerns, Tim Allen, Santa Claus, Lampoon Family Christmas Vacation, The Great Outdoors

PRICES -WHEN I WAS YOUNG:
Cost of movie - .11 cents
Comic books – .10 cents

Gasoline - .20 cents/gallon

Hair Cuts - .20 -.25 cents

Milky Way Bars -.05 cents

High Street Home was purchased for $9,000

First USED car was $50

PAID by Railroad: $1.59 ½ cents per hour

Worked at Wooden Mill before Railroad: Paid $1.29 per hour

Met Mom at dance and didn't have to pay for her -but that was .10 - .25 cents to get in.

Ice cream cones: .05 cents

Terry's Background & Memories (told to Pam)

Therese Rolande Gabouriault was born October 8, 1928 in Barre, VT. Her mother's maiden name was Merilda Allaire. Terry's memory was that her Mom was very quiet and very patient. She didn't talk much! Her father was Alphonse Gaboriault. Both of them were born in Canada, and he talked a lot! Her brothers were: Alfred, George and Roger. Her sister was Lucy. There was a 2nd baby girl "Claire' who died as a baby on Halloween.

They lived on Northfield Road, in Northfield, VT. They played baseball and loved to slide down the hill that was in their backyard in the winter. Terry shared a double bed with her sister Lucy in their bedroom that had a closet and a dresser with a chair. Terry played with the neighbor kids and loved to go the grocery store for candy. Her family went to St. Augustine Church in Montpelier. Vt. Terry's Dad worked at the Granite Shed in Barre where he polished stones. Terry's Mom stayed home and cooked and cleaned. They had a water pump to pump water in their kitchen, and Sunday's meant Roast Pork with gravy and boiled potatoes.

Her first 'story book' came from her Aunt Irene as a present. She grew up speaking French. Her first pet was a German Shepherd and they had chickens and rabbits. These were the times when women wore long dresses and hats. She got to wear pants when she went out to play. If you wanted 'ice cream' you had to make it from scratch in a churner with a handle using the icicles from off the roof.

Terry went to Grade School and then to St. Michael's High School in Montpelier. Her favorite teacher was Mrs. Williams who was from

Waterbury, VT. One of her classmates "George" would jump 'in and out' of the window to show off! Terry would work in the McClellan's Dime Store after school for .44 cents an hour and then used the money to pay the bus fare to get home and to get clothes. She loved going on a 'picnic'. Her first experience on a bike had a dog chase her and bark at her.

Her first 'crush' was on Von Law when she was 16-17 years old, and they dated. She met Trueman at a dance hall in Berlin at 19 years old. He was on leave from the Navy. He proposed 2 months after and gave her a diamond ring! They married the day after her birthday (October 8th) on October 9, 1948 at St. Augustine Church. She wore an ivory statin gown purchased in Barre. Her sister, Lucy, and Marie Brassard were her attendants, and their honeymoon was a trip to Boston and the New England States. She lived with Meme and Peppe on Northfield Road while Trueman was overseas in the Navy and went Sundays to St. Augustine Church. Her first time 'driving a car' was with Trueman, who got her to try driving. The car had a 'stick shift' and she did not like it. Terry never did get her driver's license. She loved being a 'stay at home' Mom raising the kids. She was raised to put her faith in God.

Chapter 17 -"True man" and the 1870 Book

It has been an absolute joy to have the honor to record for posterity the memories told to me by Trueman during my time spent with him in his home on the Lake. The love, care, and concern within this family for one another is a beautiful experience to behold.

As I began the 'wrap up" of this book, there was an extraordinarily rare event that occurred. As I began to finish the book, I received a gift from one of my dearest and oldest of friends, Sue.

I had visited Sue to bring her a birthday present. Before I left, she handed me a bag that contained a very old book from 1870 entitled, "Night Scenes in the Bible" by Rev. Daniel March. Knowing my last scheduled time with Trueman would be the very next day, I packed the book in my suitcase, and looked forward to taking time to read it.

Trueman Q&A

During my first day back with Trueman, I worked to obtain answers to questions contained in a book provided to me by the family entitled, "Dad Share your Life with Me". My first question to Trueman was, "Please tell me about your family names." Trueman replied, "My Dad's name was 'Charles Truman Bryer'. He did not like the name of 'Truman", so he was "Charles" and became Charles Truman. When I was born, he wanted to pass the Truman name onto me, but he did not want to spell it 'T R U M

A N'. he wanted my name to be different, so he spelled my name "True man" or "Trueman" with an 'e' in it. So, my name is "Trueman Earl Bryer". I have no idea what the Earl stands for and I don't know where the 'Earl" came from."

(Trueman's daughter Charlotte's husband, Jim, later joked, "Trueman: the "EARL" of Bryer!")

The 1870 Book

The next day when I began my Bible reading, I decided to just randomly open the 1870 book, "Night Scenes in the Bible". I opened to Chapter XVI 'A night storm on the sea" (to this excerpt):

"The ship was now in the midst of the sea, tossed with waves; for the wind was contrary. And in the fourth watch of the night Jesus went unto them, walking on the sea" (Matthew XIV 24:25).

As I read this chapter, I was totally shocked to find 'Trueman's" name in this chapter.

Excerpts from Page 354-365:

When the disciples saw Jesus' walking upon the waves, they thought they saw a spirit, an unreal and ghostly shadow, appearing to terrify rather than to comfort and deliver them. And yet he was the most true and real man that ever walked the earth. . . He is more real, true and satisfying to the earnest, thinking, aspiring mind than wealth or learning or pleasure or power. His grand purpose in all his instructions is to make us **true men** – not angels, not beings destitute of any of the passions, appetites, affections that are essential to our humanity: he would make us **true men**. He stands before us in his human nature, complete, perfect, wanting nothing. And he would make us like himself, true in every purpose, feeling and thought – true in our whole heart and soul and being. This it is to be a '**true man'**. It is to have our whole human nature purified, ennobled, consecrated by the truth. Christian faith, Christian duty, Christian character are at mortal and everlasting enmity with all pretenses, falsehood, and unreality. The man who has the most of the life of Christ in his soul is the most true, genuine and complete man on the face of the earth. . . . To be a Christian it is only necessary to be a '**true man'** – to love, believe and obey the truth." . No man can think of a more desirable close of life for himself than that he may be found faithful to his convictions, true to his own deepest sense of obligation."

My friend's Sue's History

Equally shocking is the fact that my friend Sue who gifted me the 1870's book, is the same friend who prayed in 1991 for blackberries and got 'blackberries'. She had told the Lord, ***"I do not have time to pick blackberries and if you want me to have them, you will have to give them to me!"*** The very next day, I felt compelled to go and pick 'blackberries' and then felt compelled to call Sue to ask her if she would be interested in having some blackberries. Back then, we both were awed at the power of the Lord to answer prayers.

Fast forward

NOW: After I had prayed for a way to wrap up "Trueman Bryer's Memory Book' to enable readers to understand that the Lord was honoring him, this same person, "Sue", felt compelled to gift me the 1870's book "Night Scenes in the Bible" that actually contains the message of being a 'true man' - a Trueman! My gift to her back then, now returned in full circle: Sue had prayed for 'blackberries' and I had gifted her the 'blackberries. I had prayed for this 'book' and Sue had gifted me 'a book' that condenses the entire life of a man of faith named: Trueman: Truly a 'True man".

Trueman Earl Bryer is indeed a 'true man' of FAITH and LOVE!

Life's ultimate purpose is LOVE.

We need GOD's love, present, living within us to be able to OVERCOME this world's jungle of hatred, ingratitude, discouragement, disasters, and dismays.

For it is only from God's presence within us that we can:

LOVE where there is 'hate',

FORGIVE when we are 'offended',

ENCOURAGE those who are 'discouraged'

And be a 'vessel' of the LOVE of God to others.

The letters "L – O- V - E" spell out the meaning of life:

"God is **LOVE.** (1 John 4:8)

"Beloved, let us love one another for love is of God, and everyone that loveth is of God and is known of God." (1 John 4:7)

"If any man serve me, **him** will my father honor."

Jesus (John 12:26)

"These things have I written unto you that believe on the name of the Son of God; that ye may **know** that ye have eternal life, and **that ye may**

believe on the name of the Son of God." (1 John 5:13).

"For God so loved the world that he gave his only begotten son, that whosoever believeth on him should not perish but have everlasting life. For God sent not his Son into the world to condemn the world, but that the world through him might be saved" (John 3:15-16).

"The word of faith which we preach; that if thou shalt confess with thy mouth the Lord Jesus, and shalt believe in thine heart that God has raised him from the dead, thou shalt be saved. For with the heart man believeth unto righteousness and with the mouth confession is made unto salvation" (Romans 10:9-10).

For **whosoever** shall call upon the name of the Lord shall be saved" (Romans 10:13).

Chapter 18 – Commentary by Dawn Densmore-Parent

Testimony

God is Love, God is Truth, God is Spirit. We were created to love God and to love one another. None of us can do this perfectly all the time, so from the beginning of time, a plan was devised to provide for us a way to connect with God and others.

Abraham believed God and it was counted to Him as Righteousness. Through the lineage of Abraham came Christ. The Angel Gabriel appeared to Mary and told her she would conceive by the power of the Holy Spirit and to name the baby "Jesus". Jesus was born in a manager in Bethlehem Ephratah (Micah 3:2) His ministry of serving people was for 3 and ½ years. He was delivered to Pilate the Governor of Judaea on the Jewish Passover who ordered his crucifixion on a cross with 2 other malefactors. Jesus's last statement was "It is finished" (John 19:30). The veil of the temple was rent in twain from the top to the bottom and there was a great earthquake, and the graves were opened and many bodies of the saints which slept arose and came out of the graves and went into the holy city and appeared unto many" (Matthew 27: 51-52). Nicodemus a priest and Joseph of Arimathea requested the body of Pilate and took his 'body' and placed it in Joseph's new tomb. Roman guards were sent to prevent the body from being 'stolen' because he had said after 3 days he would rise again. Early in the morning on the third day there was a great earthquake for the angel of the Lord descended and rolled back the stone from the door and sat upon it and declared to the women who came, "He is risen as He said." The guards fell to the ground and then ran away and were paid to say that his body was stolen. John and Peter went into the tomb and found the burial cloth and the napkin folded on the slab where he lay. Jesus then appeared alive for 40 days, walking through walls, eating, shewing the disciples his hands and his feet, appearing and then disappearing, until he was taken up into heaven and a cloud received him out of their sight (Acts 1:9).

The last command Jesus gave on earth was:

"Go, ye therefore, and teach all nations, baptizing them in the name of the Father and of the Son and of the Holy Ghost: Teaching them to observe all things whatsoever I have commanded you and lo, I am with you always, ***even*** unto the end of the world. Amen (Matthew 28:18-20).

www.ingramcontent.com/pod-product-compliance
Lightning Source LLC
LaVergne TN
LVHW010626100826
845148LV00014B/3133

* 9 7 8 1 7 3 4 2 3 5 3 4 0 *